I0017464

# Traffic Signal Timing

Poorly synchronised traffic signals or signal timings that do not match traffic demand can lead to inefficiencies and traffic congestions. Inadequate coordination between adjacent signals can prevent the formation of a "green wave" and cause unnecessary stops and delays for drivers.

# A Note from the Author

To all those who navigate the ever-moving currents of urban life,
To the tireless engineers, planners, and traffic management authorities,
And to the individuals whose daily journeys are shaped by the rhythm of the lights.

To the visionaries who saw the parallels between the traffic light system and Kanban,
Who recognised the power of visual cues and the significance of flow optimisation,
And who aimed to refine and perfect the art of managing both traffic and work.

# Introduction

The traffic light system and the concept of Kanban share similarities in their purpose and functioning. Kanban, which originated from the Toyota Production System, is a visual inventory control system that aims to optimise workflow and minimise waste in manufacturing and project management. Similarly, the traffic light system is designed to regulate and optimise traffic flow at intersections. By drawing parallels between these two systems, we gain insight into how both utilise visual cues and limit work in progress to improve efficiency.

Firstly, both Kanban and traffic lights emphasise the use of visual signals. In Kanban, visual cards or boards represent work items, showing their status and progress. Similarly, traffic lights use visually distinct signals to communicate with drivers and pedestrians, indicating when to stop, yield, or proceed. The clear, universally recognised colours of red, yellow, and green allow for easy comprehension and adherence to traffic rules and regulations.

Secondly, both systems limit the amount of work in progress. In Kanban, the number of work items is restricted to avoid overburdening the workers or processes. This prevents bottlenecks and helps maintain a steady workflow. Likewise, traffic lights control the number of vehicles allowed to proceed in each direction at any given time. This limitation ensures a more systematic and organised movement of vehicles, preventing gridlock and reducing the risk of accidents.

Furthermore, both systems rely on feedback loops to optimise performance. In Kanban, regular meetings or check-ins are held to review the progress of work items and identify any issues or constraints. This feedback loop allows for continuous improvement and adaptation. Similarly, traffic lights are designed to respond to changing traffic conditions. Sensors or timers detect the number of vehicles waiting, and the traffic light cycle is adjusted accordingly. This adaptive feedback mechanism enables the traffic light system to dynamically regulate traffic flow and respond to varying demands.

Lastly, both Kanban and traffic lights promote efficiency by reducing waste and improving flow. Kanban focuses on minimising idle time, reducing inventory, and eliminating unnecessary steps, leading to smoother and more efficient processes. Similarly, traffic lights optimise traffic flow by reducing unnecessary delays and minimising idle time at intersections.

The traffic light system can be likened to Kanban in terms of their visual nature, limitation on work in progress, feedback loops, and emphasis on efficiency. Both systems aim to create order, improve flow, and optimise performance. By drawing lessons from

Kanban's success in process optimisation and applying them to traffic management, we can potentially enhance the effectiveness and efficiency of the traffic light system.

## The Author

Julian Cambridge was born in London, UK.

- M.Sc. Business Computing
- B.Sc. (Hons) Computing with Business

Julian founded Golden Agile Solutions to supply IT consultancy activities to clients.

- Accredited Kanban Trainer (AKT, KMP, TKP)
- Certified Scrum Professional (CSM, CSPO, A-CSM, A-CSPO, CSP-SM)
- ICAgile Authorized Instructor (Agile Fundamentals, Agile Product Ownership, Agile Testing, Business Agility)

# The Traffic Light System

Traffic lights are carefully designed and implemented to help manage the flow of vehicles and ensure safe and efficient transportation on the roads. Traffic engineers and transportation planners utilise various principles and mathematical techniques to optimise the functioning of traffic lights.

The primary objective of traffic lights is to allocate and regulate the right-of-way for different directions of traffic at intersections. The system revolves around the control of three primary colours: red, yellow, and green. Each colour has a specific meaning and duration, and the timing of these colours is carefully calibrated.

The science behind traffic lights involves several important considerations:

1. Traffic Volumes: Traffic engineers study the traffic patterns and volumes at different times of day and days of the week to determine the appropriate signal timing. The aim is to minimise congestion and maximise traffic flow.

2. Intersection Type: The design and functioning of traffic lights vary based on the type of intersection. For example, a simple four-way intersection may use a standard cycle of red, green, and yellow signals, while a

more complex intersection with multiple turning lanes may require specific signal phasing.

3. Signal Phasing: Traffic lights follow specific signal patterns known as signal phasing. Phasing determines which movements of traffic have the right-of-way at a given time. It involves allocating time intervals for different directions of traffic, including green signal phases for specific movements and protected left turns.

4. Traffic Control Algorithms: Traffic lights employ algorithms to determine the optimal timings for each signal phase. These algorithms consider various factors, such as traffic flow, queue lengths, pedestrian crossing times, and detection of vehicles through sensors or cameras.

5. Coordination: Traffic lights can be coordinated to facilitate the movement of vehicles along a road corridor. By synchronising signal timings, engineers aim to create a "green wave" where a series of traffic lights turn green in sequence, allowing for smoother traffic flow.

6. Pedestrian Considerations: Traffic lights also prioritise pedestrian safety by allocating specific signal phases for pedestrian crossings. This allows pedestrians to safely cross the road without conflicting with vehicular traffic.

7. Adaptive Traffic Control: Advances in technology have led to the development of adaptive traffic control systems. These systems utilise real-time data from sensors and cameras to adjust signal timings dynamically based on the prevailing traffic conditions, optimising traffic flow and minimising delays.

The science behind traffic lights is continually evolving. Traffic engineers often conduct traffic modelling, simulations, and pilot studies to evaluate and improve the efficiency of signal timings. By balancing the needs of road users, traffic flow, safety, and environmental considerations, traffic light systems aim to create a more harmonious and efficient transportation network.

# Traffic Light System linked to Kanban

The traffic light system can be linked to the concept of Kanban, especially in the context of traffic management and transportation planning. Kanban, a visual system for managing workflow, originated in the manufacturing industry but has since been adapted to other fields, including project management and logistics.

In traffic management, a Kanban approach can be applied to monitor and optimise the flow of vehicles at intersections and along road networks. Here's how the traffic light system can be linked to Kanban principles:

1. Visualising Flow: Just like a Kanban board visualises the flow of work, traffic lights visually represent the flow of vehicles. Each colour of the traffic light (red, yellow, and green) communicates a specific state or action to the drivers. The visual cues provided by traffic lights help drivers understand when they have the right-of-way or need to stop.

2. Work-in-Progress (WIP) Limits: Kanban emphasises setting limits on the number of tasks in progress to avoid bottlenecks. Similarly, traffic lights impose WIP limits on the number of vehicles allowed to move through an intersection during a specific signal phase.

The duration of each phase restricts the number of vehicles that can cross, ensuring a smooth flow of traffic.

3. Queue Management: Kanban promotes reducing queues and eliminating waste. In traffic management, traffic lights regulate the formation and management of queues. By timing the traffic lights appropriately, traffic engineers aim to minimise queue lengths and waiting times for vehicles at intersections.

4. Pull System: Kanban operates as a pull system, where work is pulled based on demand and capacity. In traffic management, the movement of vehicles is also governed by a pull system. When a signal changes from red to green, it "pulls" the vehicles waiting at the intersection forward, ensuring a controlled and organised flow.

5. Continuous Improvement: Kanban encourages continuous improvement through regular reflection and adjustment. Similarly, traffic engineers regularly analyse traffic data, conduct studies, and make adjustments to signal timings to optimise traffic flow and address changing traffic patterns.

By considering traffic management within the framework of Kanban, transportation planners and traffic engineers can better visualise the flow of vehicles, set appropriate limits, manage queues efficiently, and continuously improve the overall traffic control system.

# The absence of Traffic Lights

If traffic lights are not in place at an intersection or road junction, it can lead to several challenges and potentially hazardous situations for both drivers and pedestrians. Here are some of the consequences:

1. Lack of Traffic Control: Without traffic lights, there is no official means of controlling the flow of traffic at an intersection. This can result in chaotic and unpredictable situations where multiple vehicles from different directions compete for the right-of-way simultaneously, leading to confusion and a higher risk of accidents.

2. Increased Congestion: Without traffic lights, intersections may experience more congestion, especially during peak traffic hours. Vehicles may struggle to navigate through the junction, causing delays, frustration, and longer travel times.

3. Higher Accident Rates: The absence of traffic lights can contribute to an increase in accidents. Intersections become more prone to collisions, particularly in situations where drivers are not willing to yield or when the right-of-way is unclear. Accidents can range from minor fender-benders to more severe collisions with potential injuries or fatalities.

4. Reduced Pedestrian Safety: Traffic lights usually provide designated time intervals for pedestrians to safely cross the road. Without traffic lights, pedestrians might encounter difficulties crossing intersections, making it more dangerous for them to navigate through traffic. The absence of clear rules and signals makes it harder for drivers to anticipate and yield to pedestrians.

5. Neglect of Traffic Priority: Traffic lights play a crucial role in ensuring that priority is given to the appropriate traffic flow. Without traffic lights, drivers may resort to aggressive driving or ignoring road rules, leading to confrontations and an overall disregard for traffic safety.

6. Inefficient Traffic Management: Traffic lights serve as an essential tool for transportation authorities to manage and optimise traffic flow. Without them, managing traffic effectively becomes much more challenging, as there are no control mechanisms to allocate right-of-way, adjust traffic patterns, or balance traffic volumes.

The absence of traffic lights can have significant implications for traffic control, safety, and efficiency at intersections. Implementing proper traffic control measures, including traffic lights, is crucial to maintain order, reduce accidents, and ensure the smooth flow of both vehicular and pedestrian traffic.

# Case Study: Negative

Real-life case studies where the placement of traffic lights had unintended consequences:

1. Stevens Creek Boulevard, California, USA:
In 2007, the transportation authorities in Cupertino, California, decided to install synchronised traffic lights along Stevens Creek Boulevard to improve traffic flow. However, they failed to consider the impact on pedestrian safety. The new traffic light system was designed to prioritise vehicle movement, resulting in longer crossing times for pedestrians. As a result, pedestrians faced difficulties crossing the busy road, leading to accidents and injuries. The community protested against this oversight, and the authorities eventually had to reconfigure the traffic light settings to give pedestrians adequate crossing time.

2. Portobello Road, London, UK:
In 2012, the Transport for London (TfL) introduced a new traffic light system along Portobello Road, one of London's busiest market streets. The timing of the traffic lights was intended to prioritise bus traffic, causing significant disruptions to the flow of vehicles and pedestrian movement. The removal of a pedestrian crossing added to the chaos, leading to safety concerns and frustration among local residents, traders, and visitors. The ill-conceived traffic light placement resulted

in longer travel times, increased congestion, and negative impacts on businesses. Following public outcry, TfL eventually reviewed and adjusted the traffic light timings to provide a more balanced flow for all road users.

These case studies illustrate the importance of understanding the impact of traffic light placement on all road users and the need for careful consideration of factors such as pedestrian safety, traffic flow, and community input.

While these examples highlight instances where traffic light placement had negative consequences, there are numerous successful implementations where traffic lights have greatly improved traffic management, safety, and efficiency. Proper planning, thorough analysis of traffic patterns, and effective communication play a vital role in ensuring the benefits of traffic light installations outweigh any potential drawbacks.

# Case Study: Positive

Real-life case studies where the placement of traffic lights met intended goals:

Case Study 1: London, United Kingdom –
TFL's Implementation of SCOOT System

In London, the Transport for London (TFL) implemented a traffic signal coordination system called SCOOT (Split Cycle Offset Optimisation Technique) across the city. SCOOT uses real-time traffic data and adaptive algorithms to adjust signal timings based on traffic conditions, aiming to reduce delays and improve traffic flow.

Impact: The deployment of SCOOT system resulted in significant improvements in traffic management. A study conducted by TRL (Transport Research Laboratory) found that SCOOT reduced delays at signal-controlled junctions by up to 12%, leading to smoother traffic flow and reduced journey times. Additionally, congestion levels decreased by approximately 15%, resulting in improved air quality and reduced emissions.

## Case Study 2: Munich, Germany – Traffic Light Coordination on the Mittlerer Ring

Munich implemented a comprehensive traffic light coordination system along the Mittlerer Ring, a busy circular road that encircles the city centre. The system synchronizes the signal timings of multiple intersections to create a green wave, allowing a continuous flow of traffic along this major route.

Impact: The traffic light coordination system on the Mittlerer Ring has significantly improved traffic flow and reduced congestion. Commuters traveling along this route experience smoother journeys with fewer stops at traffic lights. The synchronisation has optimised travel times for cars, buses, and bicycles, enhancing overall efficiency and promoting sustainable modes of transportation.

## Case Study 3: Toronto, Canada – Red Light Camera Program

Toronto implemented a red light camera program to improve intersection safety and discourage red light violations. Several intersections across the city were equipped with cameras that automatically capture images or videos of vehicles running red lights. Violators are then issued fines.

Impact: The red light camera program in Toronto has demonstrated positive outcomes in terms of traffic safety. According to a study conducted by the Insurance Institute for Highway Safety (IIHS), the program reduced fatal crashes caused by red light running by approximately 24%. Additionally, the presence of red light cameras has increased public awareness and compliance with traffic signals, leading to a safer driving environment.

These case studies demonstrate successful implementations of traffic light systems in real-world scenarios. By employing advanced signal coordination techniques, adaptive algorithms, and technologies like red light cameras, cities have been able to improve traffic management, reduce delays, enhance safety, and create more efficient transportation networks. These initiatives highlight the impact that well-planned and strategically placed traffic lights can have on overall traffic flow and safety.

# Summary

The traffic light system and the concept of Kanban share several similarities. Both systems rely on visual signals to communicate information, whether it is the status of work items in Kanban or the instructions for drivers and pedestrians in the traffic light system. They also limit the amount of work in progress, whether it is restricting the number of work items in Kanban or controlling the flow of vehicles at intersections through traffic lights. Both systems utilise feedback loops to continuously improve performance, whether it is through regular check-ins in Kanban or the adaptive response of traffic lights to changing traffic conditions. Additionally, both systems aim to improve efficiency by reducing waste and optimising flow.

By recognising these similarities, we can learn from the benefits of Kanban in process optimisation and apply them to enhance the effectiveness and efficiency of the traffic light system. This includes considering visual cues and clear communication, limiting congestion by controlling the number of vehicles at intersections, adapting to changing traffic patterns, and striving for continuous improvement.

Drawing upon the principles of both Kanban and the traffic light system, traffic management authorities can better regulate traffic flow, ensure safety, and minimise delays. By leveraging the power of visual cues, limiting traffic congestion, and adopting adaptive feedback mechanisms, we can strive towards creating a more efficient and orderly transportation system for the benefit of all road users.

# Foundations of Scrum Agile

Education

£2.99

App Store

Google Play

Agile Development with DevOps

Agile Project Management: Navigating Pros and Cons of Scrum, Kanban and combining them

Communication Troubles of a Scrum Team

Disney's FastPass: A Queue Story

Introducing the Douglass Model for Agile Coaches

Kaizen: The Philosophy of Continuous Improvement for Business and Education

Mastering Software Quality Assurance: A Comprehensive Guide

McDonald's: A Kanban Story

Scrum: Unveiling the Agile Method

Testing SaaS: A Comprehensive Guide to Software Testing for Cloud-Based Applications

The Art of Lean: Production Systems and Marketing Strategies in the modern era

The Board: A day-to-day feel of life on a Kanban team

The Sprint: A day-to-day feel of life on a Scrum team

The Whole Game: Systems Thinking Approach to Invasion Sports

**Traffic Light System: A Kanban Story**

www.ingramcontent.com/pod-product-compliance
Lightning Source LLC
LaVergne TN
LVHW051652050326
832903LV00034B/4823